The Mind of a Scattered Teacher

Jamie Hawthorne

BookLeaf Publishing

India | USA | UK

Presentation by *BookLeaf Publishing*

Web: www.bookleafpub.com

E-mail: info@bookleafpub.com

ISBN: 9789363317628

First edition 2024

Anatomy of a Writer

She runs on double shots of espresso
and leftover pizza.
Her hands are shaky and messy,
covered in smudged black ink.
There's bags under her eyes
from staying up all night
-not well hidden by her glasses-
Hair - not brushed
but pulled back - held up with her last spare pen.
A neatly folded napkin,
covered in scribbles,
sticking out of her shirt pocket.

Her heart beats steady
to the pace of her poetry.
Her breath - almost silent
but flows strong with the strength of the wind.

The warrior within her screams
demanding to be heard
her voice -
bounces through time and space
as she bleeds onto the page.
Unable to be ignored

She can't deny
who she is
so she'll write
until she can't write anymore.

For the Writer Within

You are a self-healing goddess that should be
worshiped by all.
You contain magnificent magic that flows from
you brain, to your heart
and out your fingertips -- finally landing onto
the page.
You move mountains, fill oceans, and shift the
winds of the very worlds that you create.
The fire and ice of your emotions quake the
earth on which your characters stand.
You are all powerful -- with creation as your
will.

You are Mother Nature.
You are Father Time.
Do not be afraid of your own power:
that of which
is fueled by words and imagination.
You are a writer.
-
In every fiber of your being.
Do not deny it, but continue to
relish in the power that you possess.
You carry an ancient strength - that
which many can only dream of.

Treat yourself with respect and patience;
Your magic…
Will follow…

My Life as a Crochet Addict

Hi my name is Jamie and i'm a crochet addict.
I'm beginning to recognize that I have a
problem.
I'm running out of room to stand In my own
bedroom.
Does my four door truck have a back seat?
I don't know - I haven't seen it in years.
Buried under bags of yarn, it probably looks
brand new.
Since it's never been sat on.

Shopping all the sales - even though I'm broke.
And I don't need any more yarn for as long as I
live.
Panic attacks at the sight of my credit card bills
Not getting a cart so i don't spend too much
But spending too much anyway.
Getting dirty looks from the people in the check
out line
As my yarn avalanches out of my arms and rolls
three aisles away.
The shock on the cashiers face when I plop all
my items on the counter,
Opening up my arms like I'm releasing a bear
hug.

I've been making a habit out of
Forgetting to write down the pattern as i go -
Only making one and not knowing how I did it.
Then never making another one
Because it's too much effort to figure out
After not remembering how I did it the first
time.

The look on my fiance's face when he sees me
pick up my yarn
And realizing he won't be getting any tonight.
Complaining about not getting enough sleep
But not being willing to crochet for one less
hour.
The irritation of working on a project for almost
all night, then realizing
I've used the wrong hook size and need to start
over.

Hi my name is Jamie and I'm a crochet addict.

I Wish To Be

I wish to be confident
in all things I do.

I wish to be great
at the things I enjoy.

I wish to be loved
by those most important.

I wish to be happy
in all aspects of my life.

I wish to be truly me
and not lose myself
in the madness of the world.

I Am From

I am from the space between the pen and paper.
I dwell here, floating in the undried ink.
I bleed words and cry literature.
My journal is my best friend.

Pixie Hollow is my home.
I am from the scattered mess of my workshop.
I spend hours upon hours there -
So much so - that I forget to go outside to smell
the roses.

I am part of the tide.
The water runs through my veins and flows
through my thoughts.
I am from the ocean.
The waves sooth my body,
while the current washes away the stress of my
day.

My heart beats like a strong base drum.
I hear the keys of the piano.
I constantly feel the strumming of the guitar.
I am from the fluidity of music.

My strength comes from tough love -
The power of my will comes from my
experiences.
I am from my trauma -
I am from my journey -
I am from the universe.

Not Responsible

I am not responsible for
the way stupid people drive
or where bees build their hive.

I am not responsible for
the rain
or your pain.

I am not responsible for
how you chose to treat me
or how you take your coffee.

I am only responsible for
my own happiness.
And I am happy with that.

Forgot to Stop for Gas

Running on fumes -
The gas tank is empty,
lights on and blinking,
My car's telling me she's hungry.

My coffee cup's empty -
there's only a drop left,
and it's cold.
Uh oh, here comes a yawn.

We both could have used a refill - but
I forgot to stop for gas.

When I'm Tired

12

Gods help the stupid people
who mess with me
before I've had my coffee.

No energy, no patience, no sympathy.

Gods help the stupid people
who mess with me
before I've had my coffee.

Make Me a Sandwich

Make me a sandwich,
And let me eat it.

Bring it to my lair,
Where all things crocheted and
Of poetic line are born.

Make me a sandwich,
For I, the Tinker, requite sustenance
To get me through my current poem.

Make me a sandwich
So that when I am done devouring it,
I may devour you
Instead.

Just Because

Just because I am a girl
Does not mean that I like pick or prefer ballet;
Doesn't mean that I am physically weak,
And does not mean I belong in a kitchen
Or am more comfortable in a skirt.

I am a warrior.

Just because I am sick
Doesn't mean that I am incapable,
Does not mean that you get to treat me like I
have the plague,
And doesn't mean that I'm always in need of
help.

I am a fighter.

Just because I am blonde
Doesn't mean I'm an airhead;
No, I am not a ditz or a Barbie.
I am not stupid or self-centered.

I am a smart woman and a published writer.

Just because I go to therapy
Does not mean that I am broken or damaged;
I am not weak.

I am a survivor.

Princess

Before I start with Once Upon a Time -
let's get one thing clear.
Pumpkins can't turn into carriages and glass
slippers will never fit.
There are no strokes of midnight and fairy
godmothers just don't exist.
Singing dwarves won't come to save you
and a kiss won't awaken the beauty.

We live in a world without magic
- where happy endings are a fallacy, but
somehow
There's a poisoned apple on every tree
and we're all still trapped in towers
- forever.

Wouldn't it be nice if the princess wasn't the
damsel in distress?
Maybe in this world, it's true.

The dragons have become my family
And the dragon slayers are now the enemy.
Because here I am,
with my bow and arrows
ready to take back my kingdom
from my villains.

We find magic in our own world because we
know exactly where to look.
Now,
Once Upon a Time …
I was the rightful queen of my life.

Vows to Myself

Now and forever,
I will love myself.
With this ring, I place upon my finger;
A symbol of my commitment
to the task of treating myself
with respect and love.
I vow to care for my body, mind,
and spirit
by doing all I can
to keep me happy.
I recognize my flaws,
change what I can,
and embrace what I can't.
I need to love myself
just as much - if not more
than he loves me.

I need to get out of my own way
Let go of insecurities and frustrations
break through the barriers I've built around me
He's already bulldozed most of it
Now it's time for me to take a sledgehammer to
the rest.

Pacing Time

What is the matter with Time?
Can it please choose a steady pace
And just stick to it?
Why did time speed up - to make
Two years - feel like yesterday?

Sooner than you realize,
You'll be here
Then, maybe - but just maybe
Time might stop - only
For a moment.

In the blink of an eye,
I'll miss a couple years once more
Time will be going even faster
Than before.
Time has no intention of stopping
To give us a break or let us take
A breath.
Or even to let us enjoy this wonderful
Moment - that is fast approaching.

What will happen in this moment?
Will Father Time pause the clocks?

Untitled

I stay awake as the nights tick by,
yet people slumber soundly.
I'm drowning at the waters' edge,
surrounded by swirling papers -
coming in and out with the tides.
Letters float all around me;
my brain can't catch them in time -
My hand - unable to keep up.
They slip between my fingers
as easily as the oceans' waves.
I contemplate the troubling sway of my
thoughts.
Sleep continues to escape me.
For words come only as moments,
but last for all eternity.

Tattoo Therapy

21

......

The only socially acceptable
version of cutting yourself.

The Call

I hear it calling.
The scream is undeniable.
Visions in my thoughts,
showing me its purpose.
The refreshing warmth -
pours over my entire body,
drenching every inch of me.
It wipes away my frustration…
Every day that it falls from the sky -
it screams my name even louder!
The call becomes harder to
ignore…
I need it like air in my lungs.
I'm waiting for my time -
The day I can walk out,
into the rain,
and never look back.

Recipe for Disaster

1 cup of lies
2 sprinkles of self doubt
A pinch of regret
2 tablespoons of "whoops"
A splash of FUCK's
add a whole lemon zest - for flavor

Mix together , bake in oven at 325 degrees for
45 minutes.

Let cool, cut and enjoy.

Love

The flowers giggle when Love is planted.
The trees smile when Love is harvested.
The fruits grove when Love is watered.
And in the heart of Love, lies truth.
Infinite, is this truth.

This truth pounds down the walls of the heart
to smother the heart in a pool of love.
The good, the bad, and the ugly -
all walk into Love's arms.
Love accepts all and all live
within Love's heart.
Unconditional love brews goodness
within your home together.
For Home is where you hang your heart;
where the souls are blessed - chosen to be
family,
find their eternal peace with each other.

Unconditional love has no walls,
but is an abyss of rebirth and light in the heart.
It is acceptance, wisdom, understanding,
and strength. It is the
guidance for you to carry with your
within your minds, bodies, and souls;
to use for the rest of your lives.

Feeling the Inspiration

Feeling the inspiration
Like a big jolt of energy
The warmth of a fire on a cold night
Or the ocean on a 100 degree day at the beach
My hand can't stop
Can't read my handwriting anymore

Feeling the inspiration
Taking me away
Like flying on a cloud
Catching my thoughts in jars
Like fireflies on a summer night
Electricity on my finger tips

Writing like the energizer bunny
Pounding on his drum
As he glides across the floor

Inspiration comes and goes.
Gone more often than here with me
But I feel it.

Sleeplessness

As I lie awake thinking
Dreaming of dragon embers
Until then, when I remember
My thoughts and stories, and I still, never
blinking.

Absence of Chaos

27

The silent humming of tranquility…
Not light - not dark,
Just existing
and fading away -
all at once.